To our Denton family. I love you and hope these pages will be a blessing to you as your.

Love,
Nancy Pierce

Moments of Reflection

Nancy Pierce

Inspiring Voices
A Service of **Guideposts**

Inspiring Voices books may be ordered through booksellers or by contacting:

Inspiring Voices
1663 Liberty Drive
Bloomington, IN 47403
www.inspiringvoices.com
1-(866) 697-5313

ISBN: 978-1-4624-0514-5 (sc)
ISBN: 978-1-4624-0515-2 (e)

Printed in the United States of America

Inspiring Voices rev. date: 03/01/2013

Table of Contents

Moments of Reflection

Moments of Reflection

(All Scriptures, unless otherwise noted, are from the New King
James Version)

Poems, Essays, and Songs by Nancy Pierce
Music by Araceli Cavazos
Cover Photo by Morton Photographic Arts

Preface

Through the years, as I have read my Bible or listened to a teaching or sermon, words for a poem or ideas for an essay would begin to form in my mind. Sometimes it would be during a time of admiring God's creation in all things around me. As soon as I could find a piece of paper and pen or pencil, I would begin writing. Sometimes it was on a scrap of paper, a napkin, or a church bulletin or it might be an actual page in a notebook. In many situations, I felt God guiding me to use the gift of writing that He had given to me. It is to His glory that I have been encouraged to put these words in print to share with whoever will read them.

At many times in our lives we seek to know what to do or say, or we seek comfort, and God's word is our way to faith, comfort, and joy to carry on in our lives day by day. Sometimes we just need to express our appreciation to Him for being present or for painting a beautiful picture in nature for us to enjoy. Through these writings, I have attempted to show Him my love in return for all that His word and His world have given to me.

Whether we are going through painful changes in our lives or walking on a smooth road, we can have faith that He will bring us through the changes in His time and we can hope it is all for our good. In Romans 8:28, we can read that "All things work together for good to those who love God, to those who are the called according to His purpose." It is my hope that all who read these works will be blessed and encouraged in the faith and hope He gives to live in peace and joy in every circumstance.

Our Father's World

The Beginning

I like to watch the world change at dawn,

When with the greater light of the sun,

The stars begin to disappear into heaven

To await their turn to shine again,

Keeping watch another night.

The hues of sky and earth are streaked

With the interchanging lights:

Night blue to mauve, then morning red

At the horizon,

While the higher dome prepares

For the light beams to reach up and paint it too.

Shadows begin to put on life,

And finally I see them for what they are.

I wonder if this is how it looked

When God's creation settled down into the day

When there was first light.

My Lord's Day

Psalm 118: 24—This is the day the Lord has made; we will rejoice and be glad in it.

Mark 11:24–26 — "Therefore, I say to you, whatever things you ask when you pray, believe that you receive them, and you will have them.

"And whenever you stand praying, if you have anything against anyone, forgive him that your Father in heaven may also forgive you your trespasses.

"But if you do not forgive, neither will your Father in heaven forgive your trespasses."

> Today is the day my Lord has made,
>
> And through whatever this day may hold,
>
> I know that He loves me
>
> And always is near,
>
> So in praise to Him I'll be bold!
>
> No half-hearted thank-you will I offer to Him

Nor shy little voice in shame;

But I'll open my heart,

And I'll open my mouth

And sing loud hallelujahs to His name!

If I ask for things in line with His will,

Just as He promised me,

He'll answer my prayer,

And not a thing withhold.

What wonders I will see!

But first I must go and forgive anyone

Against whom I hold ill will

Then my heart will be free

To accept His grace

My cup filled 'til it starts to spill.

Yes, today is the day my Lord has made,

And it is good, for it is His.

He's prepared the way

For me to go,

And I shall be glad in it as it is.

A Speck of Dust

This poem was written in 1977, when I was a teenager and it was my first "published" work. It found its way into a group of student-created poems and essays that were chosen each year and stored in the school library for people to read. I felt a great deal of pride and excitement to be chosen. Since I was a teenager, I wasn't really knowledgeable about the facts on gold and how it was formed and found, but it made sense to me at the time and no one tried to correct my non-researched ideas. It may have been my first real attempt at writing poetry. Because of that, I have decided to include it here.

Here is a speck of dust from a nugget of gold.

Who knows it has fallen here?

Would anyone perceive it among the sands?

It is lost, abiding with acquaintances, yet strangers,

A speck of dust and a million grains of sand.

There is One who knows its worth;

No matter that it glitters not even so
much as the sand that surrounds it,

Nor that it is buried deep by someone's
great and heavy strides

There is One who will find it, know it, and make it grow.

He takes up the million grains of sand

And sifts them through His great fingers.

There remains in His palm but
one small dull mite;

The rest escaped.

He gazes at that one and knows
where there are others like it.

He holds it gently while He
searches out the others.

He finds them, seeing them where they lie.

He puts them in His hand, each dusty mite,

And together they grow slowly, slowly,

Until they are one beautiful rock, a nugget of gold!

God's Appointed Caretaker

___A Prayer

Genesis 1:27–28 — So God created man in His own image; in the image of God He created him; male and female He created them. Then God blessed them, and God said to them, "Be fruitful and multiply; fill the earth and subdue it; have dominion over the fish of the sea, over the birds of the air, and over every living thing that moves on the earth."

Genesis 9:1–3—So God blessed Noah and his sons, and said to them: "Be fruitful and multiply, and fill the earth. And the fear of you and the dread of you shall be on every beast of the earth, on every bird of the air, on all that move on the earth, and on all the fish of the sea. They are given into your hand. Every moving thing that lives shall be food for you. I have given you all things, even as the green herbs."

I am here through Thy grace;

By Thy grace here I live and work and play.

Thou hast deeded me a portion

Of Thy world to care for day by day.

Help me to keep my portion as Thou would

So that when I turn it back to Thee,

It will be as beautiful and good

As it started out to be.

Amen

The flowers appear on the earth; the time of singing has come, and the voice of the turtledove is heard in our land.
—Song of Solomon 2:12

God's Resources

_A contemplation

There are three "natural" resources I think about, which will never be diminished:

> God's love is <u>fuel</u> to warm us and keep us going.

> God's forgiveness is the <u>oil</u> to soothe our ailments.

> God's kindness is the <u>space</u> that will
> always be comfortable.

These resources of God should be tapped into and used daily in order to keep them in highest production. By sharing them, we uncover even more of each of them, and the more of them we uncover, the more bountiful they grow.

What Is the Church?

The church is

Concerned disciples of Jesus Christ

Having one hope together,

Uplifted by God's grace,

Responding to His love,

Carrying the Gospel to others through the

Holy Spirit's power

Becoming a Butterfly

_A little story

Butterflies, moths, so many different kinds, and all have become the beautiful creatures they are through the same miraculous process. The final stage in their creation is something to make one marvel when considering what the graceful creatures were at the beginning of their lives. I imagine it would go something like this.

"Mm-m. Oh! What's going on? What brightness! What has happened?" A small creature, a caterpillar, comes slowly out of a tiny bulb-like egg and is dazed at first, at her surroundings. But then, soon, as she becomes accustomed to the light, she decides, "Well, this might not be so bad." She begins to chew at her little shell and comments to herself, "Hm-m, in fact, that tastes pretty good. Yes, VERY good!"

But no sooner has she eaten the shell she just emerged from and begun to enjoy a meal of the fresh green leaf she finds herself upon than suddenly, she finds herself choking, then becoming slightly dazed and weak, and falls to the ground.

"Oomph!" she gasps, "What hit me? It was, uh, wet. Yes, that was it. It was very wet and cold. I didn't like it at all and now here I am down on the ground and I feel terrible. Maybe if I just rest a while, my mind will clear up and my legs will feel stronger."

Soon, with the rapidly warming air from a bright morning sun, the caterpillar begins to feel her strength returning and as she rests and waits for the numbness to leave her many legs, she begins to ponder this strange life in which she finds herself.

"I don't know what that was all about, but I'd almost rather go back into that shell I just ate."

About that time, a beautiful and graceful creature settles on the leaf above the young caterpillar.

"My goodness, you look like you just had a small dose of yard and garden spray. How do you feel?" asks the creature.

"Terrible! What's 'yard and garden spray'?"

"Dear little one, you've come into a man's world, and he doesn't take kindly to your feeding on the plants that he thinks he has caused to grow here. He's always coming around with this can of stuff called 'yard and garden spray,' about once a week on average, wetting the whole place down with it. And it's murder on us insects." The creature slowly exercises its wings as it talks, and the caterpillar watches its grace and beauty as she is beginning to feel good at just having someone around who seems to know what things are all about, especially such a pleasant someone.

"You seem to know about what I've been through," she notes. "Can you tell me if it's going to be this way all along? Because, if it is, I'd just as soon that stuff had got me once and for all as to have to go through this misery again."

"Oh, no, don't feel that way!" the creature quickly flutters down beside the homely little caterpillar. "You've come through this quite well. I know it isn't pleasant. The same thing happened to me when I was a caterpillar. Luckily, the mixture was down to almost pure water when it hit the leaf I was on, and it seems to have been the same for you."

"Wait a minute. You were a caterpillar?" Disbelief shows on the little fuzzy face. "But you couldn't have been. Look at you—you're beautiful, and so sure of yourself."

"Oh, yes," replies the creature, "I was a caterpillar and I felt just like you. But a butterfly (that's what I am, by the way) used to come to get nectar from the flowers of the plant where I ate, and she helped me to see what I could look forward to if I'd just be patient through my caterpillar stage."

Again, "Wait, wait, wait a minute," interrupts the caterpillar. "Just hold on! Back up. You lost me back there at you being a–what is it? a 'flutter by'?"

"No," laughs the butterfly. "I am a butterfly."

"Oh. Well, you look more like a flutter by. Anyway, is that your name? Butterfly? And what were you talking about?"

"No. I AM a butterfly. My name is Royal. I'm of the monarch variety. You look like you might become a swallowtail. If so, you're really going to glorify your Creator."

"Now, there you go again. Would you mind telling me what you're talking about? But wait until I crawl up on that leaf where I can see you better. It seems quite dry. I think the man missed this plant for some reason."

As the caterpillar crawls slowly up the plant stem and onto the leaf, Royal flutters up and lights easily on the flower next to the leaf. She sips a little nectar from the bloom and then begins.

"All right. I'll explain. You've already found out that life isn't just one long easy meal of fresh green leaves. Just when you think you've got the whole plant to yourself something comes along to remind you that you're not the only bug in the garden. You'll run into a number of enemies. Sometimes even those who look like they should be friends will turn out to be your worst enemies.

"But every time you meet one of them and survive the meeting, you'll be that much stronger and that much wiser."

"Oh, sure," sneers the caterpillar, "and how much joy is there in being a strong, wise, and dead caterpillar?"

"Well, all I can tell you now," says Royal, "is that the stronger and wiser you grow, the more joy you will feel in everything. Even in being a caterpillar for the time. And your Creator will be with you along the way, up to and beyond becoming a butterfly."

Suddenly Royal flutters quickly up as she calls back to the caterpillar, "Oh, oh! There come the children. I have to fly away for now. They'd like to pin me to a board and look at me dead on their wall. So I'll have to fly off to stay free. They don't yet understand how much more they can enjoy me alive than dead. I'll loop some loops to entertain them, then land well above their reach so they can still see me, but cannot touch me. I'd advise you to get to the underside of that leaf you're on. They like to collect caterpillars in jars to see if you'll weave a cocoon while they watch until you hatch from that into a butterfly."

At this, the caterpillar and the butterfly part ways. But it's not without the caterpillar beginning to wonder at this world she has entered into, in which an ugly creature like herself can go to sleep one day and wake up as a totally different creature. And to think she might wake up some day as beautiful as her new friend Royal.

And this Creator that Royal spoke of, she wants to find out more about this too. As she crawls to a safer place while the children are wandering in the garden, she thinks of all she has learned and begins to be full of hope, first that this Creator will protect her, and second that she will someday be a beautiful creature like Royal.

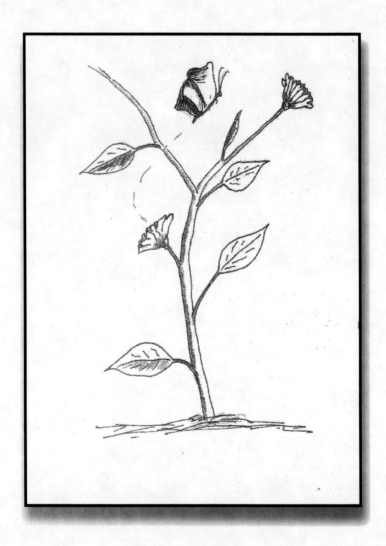

A Few Essays
Inspired by Personal Experience, Observation and God's Word

A Meditation on Hope

When I read a novel or watch a movie that I thoroughly enjoy, I become so engrossed in the story and characters that I often find myself living the story in my imagination so that I perceive events and ideas as though they were mine. In that imagination, hope for a happy conclusion to the conflicts of the characters stays uppermost in my mind. Usually, just about the time one problem seems on the verge of being resolved, something comes along to hinder that. Problem after problem comes along in this way, but I am always sure that by the time I reach the end of the story, the conflict will be resolved in one way or another. The outcome depends partly on circumstances and partly on decisions of the characters.

Reading through these stories, on some pages I feel an expectancy that something good is just around the corner, a step toward a happy conclusion. However, at other points, I feel suspense and frustration about what is ahead because it seems that no good could result after a certain chain of events or decisions. No matter how I feel at different points in the story, I always have hope that in the very end, it will all come together for a satisfactory ending. Yet, I've read some stories in which that doesn't happen and I am terribly disappointed. The characters just never quite get the hang of what is causing all their problems, nor do they learn how to handle those problems forced upon them by others. I think most people like stories in which good overcomes evil. Most of us probably feel the same way concerning real life.

In life, the conflicts, suspenseful chains of events, and moments of joyful expectation are there for each one of us. Unlike in stories, though, we can have a well-founded hope for a completely happy ending. As Paul says in Romans 8:25, "But if we hope for what we do not see, we eagerly wait for it with perseverance." Where is this kind of hope based? In spite of wrong turns and unwise choices, there is a condition under which we can be sure that in the very end of things all will come together for our good. It is as simple as making one very important right choice at one point along the way. Once we have made that choice, and as long as we never back away from it, there is nothing else that can keep us from that final victorious conclusion when the story of our life is finished.

None of us will ever live without making mistakes in what we think, do, or say. We can't escape the world's troubles brought about by sinful humans. God, who made us, knows all about us and our imperfect ways, yet He, in His perfect love, provided a way for us to attain a wonderful ending to all of the messes we make for ourselves throughout life. In believing God's provision, then, by making one right decision, and finally, living in patient expectation (hope), our shining, victorious conclusion will obliterate any adversity along the way.

Look at God's provision in John 3:16. "For God so loved the world [sinful though we may be] that He gave His only begotten Son, that whoever believes in Him should not perish but have everlasting life." That is our first ray of hope.

Next, we have to make that one right decision, as we see in Romans 10:9. "...If you confess with your mouth the Lord Jesus [that He is the Son of God and Lord of my life who died in my place for all my past, present, and future sins] and believe in your heart that God has raised Him from the dead, you will be saved [the good ending]." This confession of belief and statement of the results of believing is the second ray of hope.

Finally, with Jesus in our hearts and His Spirit's guidance, we can live in the expectation stated in James 5: 7–8. "Therefore, be patient, brethren, until the coming of the Lord. See how the farmer waits for the precious fruit of the earth, waiting patiently for it until it receives the early and latter rain. You also be patient. Establish your hearts, for the coming of the Lord is at hand." This is living the hope.

With these thoughts in mind, there need be no fear of things here or things to come. To some who refuse to accept God's provision, make the decision, and watch expectantly for His wondrous ending, this is foolish talk. But foolish as it may sound to some, what has anyone to lose by taking those three steps? Only a life of fear here and a life of eternal suffering after this one is over. Even for those who believe they will just die and be in oblivion as they return to dust, wouldn't it be great to at least try this way and find, in the end, that after all the world puts us through here, we could live an eternity in good health, with no suffering of any kind, in the presence of Someone who loves us more than we could ever imagine? We won't escape suffering here; Satan has seen to that, but anyone should be willing to take the chance that what these verses in the Bible say is true. Put it to the test; you will be pleasantly surprised at the results, even in this life, as you feel peace in spite of what the world does to you. Hope for the best.

Whose Map Do You Follow?

Psalm 18:8 — It is better to trust in the Lord than to put confidence in man.

Look to God for your needs and not to the world, for the false god of the world will surely give you one thing by cheating you out of another. But with God, He has promised you everything, asking nothing in return except that you believe in His Son, whom He gave up to death on the cross for you. If it seems God isn't answering you, look into yourself and search out your real motives: have you desired to go with Him or with the world? If you have desired the ways of the world, then don't look to God to fill your needs; ask the world for them since that is what you are worshiping. On the other hand, if you find upon self-examination that you have truly desired God's will in a matter, then patience is the key. Never quit hoping, and always keep walking according to the way He shows you, a step at a time.

All you need to know of the future is that, if you have given it all over to His plan, He has it in safe keeping. With that in mind, you can take what each day brings and look on it as another step, another turn in the road, a little less distance to the goal He has set for you.

Each road to each part of your future does come to a destination. If you have let God guide your way, you will reach those places in time. These little accomplishments are like rest stops; they are good and we can be thankful for them. Then we start off again toward other goals until reaching the ultimate stop in heaven, knowing there will be some rough roads on the way, but still with some rest stops to bask in God's goodness. And while we are on the road between rest stops, He shows us evidence of Himself with us everywhere we look, if we will but look, evidence that we are not on this road alone and that we are not lost.

Even if you have followed the world's map for your life's desires up to now, God is still ready and waiting to present you with his plans for you. Let Him know you are willing to accept what He has already done for you through His Son and that you are ready to make your journey using His map.

Eternity: Where?

Scriptural references:
Galatians 6:8; Daniel 12:2; John 5:28-29; John 6:40;
Romans 3:23-25

God's mercy and forgiveness are there for us as long as we live. However, once this flesh of ours dies, our last breath will have been our last chance to ask for and accept that forgiveness. If there were nothing alive about us except our flesh and bones, then death would be the end, but we are spirit, too, and our spirit doesn't die. If the spirit of evil and disgrace has been the spirit we have kept alive within our flesh, then that's the spirit that stays alive until a second death. But if we have let the Spirit of God fill us, of course that is the part of us that will live on. As we live here on earth, we have the choice of following our own sinful spirit or the Holy Spirit of God. It is that very decision, which can be only ours and which determines where and how life after death will be.

As I understand the Scriptures, after death our spirits will take on new bodies and they will be able to feel and react to our surroundings. These spirits will either live on in the unbearable surroundings described as hades or in the ideal and beautiful atmosphere of heaven. This is one thing we are not allowed to sample before making a decision. We have to read, understand, and believe what God is telling us about it in His word, in the Scriptures.

First of all, we have to know in our hearts that Jesus is real and that the story of His sacrifice on the cross and His resurrection is true. After that, we must acknowledge that we are all sinners; no one is perfect. Then we have to openly confess this fact about our lives and be sincerely sorry about it. Next, God will forgive when we ask Him to. If all of these acts come from our hearts, we should soon notice that we desire a new way of living. Still we are not perfect, but now when we sin, we again repent and ask for forgiveness and God blots out all sins we have committed, past and present. Now we continue to grow and desire to walk in God's way because we have acknowledged our belief that Jesus died for us and that we are forgiven sinners because of that. But all the while, we are trying, with His help, to live in obedience to Him. Finally, we will be assured of spending eternity with Him in heaven, where "God will wipe away every tear from their eyes; there shall be no more death, nor sorrow, nor crying. There shall be no more pain, for the former things have passed away." This is the eternity that I choose.

God's Faithfulness

Scriptures: Psalm 37:3-5; I Thessalonians 5:16-18

I have heard a few people who say, "Well, I used to pray and believe in God to help me. But one time when I really needed His help, He never came through. So I have given up on Him. I no longer believe He answers prayer, so I don't bother to pray anymore. If He loves me so much, why did He let me down? I just take care of myself now."

This philosophy is hard for me to understand. First of all, God never lets us down even though there are times it seems to our minds that He has. It is all a matter of how patient we are in waiting for Him to act and also of realizing that a loving Father sometimes has to say no when He knows a thing is not the best for us to have or when our motivation for our request is the wrong one. Many times we might not even realize that He actually has answered, but not with the answer we thought He should give.

How many of us have had a favored car or appliance that we really hated to let go of? Month after month, the engine of the old heap or the motor of the old appliance fails, usually at the worst possible moment. Nonetheless, we are willing to pour money and time into fixing it up, always hoping that this time we have fixed it for good, that now it will serve us faithfully. As long as we are willing to keep putting in new parts, repairing old ones, and spending a lot of time and money on it, it will keep going for a fairly long time.

On the other hand, how many of us have given up on God because we have put in time and money and patience through prayer, reading the Scriptures, giving financially to His "repair shop," yet we don't get what we ask for? God doesn't need us to keep his world going, but we need Him to keep ours going. We are the ones who need that same kind of faith focused on God that we show toward our ability to keep some of our earthly possessions in working condition. Through our willingness to spend whatever we need to in time, energy, or money, we keep those possessions serving our needs. Real enduring, untiring faith in that object is rewarded. Nevertheless, with all our efforts, that machine will someday give out and fail us for good. But God never will. As long as we stay in there, never giving up, always hoping and looking for His answer, whatever it may be, we will finally be rewarded with it and it won't be some temporary adjustment. We are our own most important machine, and God is our exclusive repairman, but we have to spend a lot of time in His shop to be in top running condition at all times. If we don't spend that time with Him, learning to live in obedience to Him, meditating on all the ways He has blessed us already, then we cannot blame God when it seems our prayers go unanswered. We can only blame our lack of trust in Him to keep His promises and to do what is best in each circumstance of our lives. Giving up on Him may be quitting just when the answer is right around the corner.

God's Spirit in Us

Matthew 26:36 — Peter said to Him, "Even if I have to die with you, I will not deny you." And all the other disciples said the same.

Matthew 26:40–41—Then He returned to the disciples and found them sleeping and said to Peter, "What! Could you not watch with Me one hour? Watch and pray lest you enter into temptation. The spirit is willing, but the flesh is weak."

Matthew 7:7–8 — "Ask, and it will be given to you; seek, and you will find; knock, and it will be opened to you. For everyone who asks receives; and he who seeks finds; and to him who knocks, it will be opened."

[Continue to read *Matthew 7:9–11, Matthew 26:69–75, and Acts 2:10 and 21*]

Until we are filled with God's Holy Spirit, we do not have it within ourselves (mind or body) to be really committed to God. We want to be, as Peter and the other disciples did, but on our own, we can't be. It takes His Spirit within us for us to be what God wants us to be. Therefore, seek His filling of our hearts with His Spirit. Only God can do this for us, and if we simply ask, as Jesus promised, it will be done for us.

After Peter was filled with the Spirit at Pentecost, he went on to do exactly what he had claimed he would in Matthew 26:36. As we read, before that inner filling, he had gone away in shame and guilt, realizing he was not able to live up to his words.

If we sincerely ask for God's Spirit to dwell in us, He will give us what we ask for. The wonderful changes in our lives, sometimes immediately or sometimes gradually over time, will be evidence of God's answer to our prayer. The power that turned Peter, who was an uneducated fisherman when Jesus first called him, into a man who spoke easily to the crowd in Jerusalem, boldly telling them that "whoever calls on the name of the Lord shall be saved" can be ours. He went on to heal a crippled beggar, causing people to be "all amazed and perplexed, saying to one another, 'Whatever could this mean?'" After that, Peter continued to preach and heal as he and the other apostles went all over their world, preaching and teaching the Gospel, healing and standing up for their faith, and finally giving up their lives for their faith.

Men, who once had been afraid to acknowledge Jesus as their leader when confronted with the danger of doing so, did a 180 degree turn to become men who were willing to die in spreading God's word about Jesus as the Son of God.

We also will surprise ourselves, and probably others, at what our lives can be like once we have acknowledged our need for God to forgive us for all our sins, when we accept that Jesus, God's only Son, died for us so that God would forgive us, and finally, when we invite him to fill our hearts with His Spirit. We and others will be amazed, and maybe perplexed, saying "What does this mean?" about what has happened to us.

Reflections on the Ways of Life through the Years

God Has Filled Me

God has allowed me fulfillment

In so many different ways.

As daughter, wife, and mother

Throughout my early days;

As sister, teacher, grandmother,

For these, too, I give Him praise.

And still He keeps on adding

More ways to use His gifts,

More ways to share His blessings,

More ways my praises lift.

And now in these later days

He still uses me, as I grow,

To let His light shine through me,

To forever let His love flow,

To open my heart to others

So His kindness in me shows.

A Changing of Life Styles

1976 — in my middle years

My life is being repaired and renovated. Sometimes when something needs to be sawed and hammered, it hurts terribly. But the new look when it is finished will cause the strain and pain of it all to be soon forgotten.

1981 — adding a few years

God's renovation is still going on. As I look back on what he's done so far, considering the broken down shambles this life was, I'm glad to know the Master Builder is working on me. He has taken out many strained and warped boards and added new ones to his foundation that was there to start with. Now there is less hammering and sawing. The inside painting, papering, and decorating are going on. I love the way it feels. I can hardly wait for the landscaping!

2012 — Many years later

Who knows how many years I have left? But whatever I have, I feel the overhaul job on my life is nearing completion because the landscaping is well along. The repairs and interior decorating still need a little touching up now and then, but it is a lot less painful. When I maintain myself as I should, fewer touch-ups are required. The landscaping has been interesting. As some things on the outside begin to fade out, the Master Gardener has brightened up the landscape by planting smiles and blooms of joy, protection from strong winds by calm thoughts covering me all over. Then there is the cooling fountain of living water added by the Master Gardener's capable Assistant.

I am becoming a living home for His Spirit under the Master Builder's hand and the blooms in my garden, under His care, will never fade away.

John 3:

There was a man of the Pharisees named Nicodemus, a ruler of the Jews. 2) This man came to Jesus by night and said to Him, "Rabbi, we know that You are a teacher come from God; for no one can do these signs that You do unless God is with him."

3) Jesus answered and said to him, "Most assuredly, I say to you, unless one is born again, he cannot see the kingdom of God."

5) Jesus answered, "Most assuredly, I say to you, unless one is born of water and the Spirit, he cannot enter the kingdom of God. 6) That which is born of the flesh is flesh, and that which is born of the Spirit is spirit. 7) Do not marvel that I said to you, "You must be born again."

Spiritual Waters

I am a well, deep and full.

    Inside of me are stored waters

    Of love, compassion, and service.

Sometimes I almost run dry

After having my waters scooped out

    again and again

    to serve to people who need them.

When I grow nearly empty,

    God sends down His Spirit

    refilling and replenishing.

Sometimes I hide myself under a cover

    of selfishness, pride, and anger,

    in darkness deep down inside.

So that I am not able

> to receive the sweet water

> He rains down to fill me.

Then God patiently lifts off my cover

> and gently begins to fill me

> with living waters again.

Other times, my waters lie deep within me

> so still and undisturbed

> growing stagnant and useless.

Then God carefully clears away

> the filthy debris

> that has collected

And stirs up new life inside

> within the depths

> of my soul

Until my waters bubble up

> fresh and ready

> to give of themselves again.

And God Said

Lord, some say You don't speak to us in a voice anymore.

But I have heard You speak that way many times.

Not in the sound of the wind,

> or the roar of the ocean,

> or the songs of birds.

These are Your creations, Lord,

And You do speak through the beauty of their sounds.

But I have heard You speak to me in words,

In the voice of man.

> You have spoken to me:

>> through someone's voice lifted
>> in songs of praise to You;

>> through the voice of a friend
>> speaking comforting words;

through the voice of a child quoting
memorized Bible verses or singing

"Jesus loves me;"

through the voice of my
husband saying, "I love you;"

through the voice of my son or
daughter saying, "Mom, I'm home!"

through the voice of a parent
saying, "I'm proud of you."

Through many voices, Lord,
Your words come to me,

Reminding me of Your presence
everywhere in my life,

encouraging me,

loving me,

filling me with joy,

rewarding my faith.

I'm grateful for Your speaking to me in
voices with words I can understand.

On Matthew 18:12-14

The Scripture: [These are Jesus' words.]

Matthew 18:12) "What do you think? If a man has a hundred sheep, and one of them goes astray, does he not leave the ninety-nine and go to the mountains to seek the one that is straying? 13)And if he should find it, assuredly I say to you, he rejoices more over that sheep than over the ninety-nine that did not go astray. 14)Even so it is not the will of your Father who is in heaven that one of these little ones perish."

Reflection

I see around me

not one, but many, who are lost,

and whether all of those

or only one be found,

Our Father in heaven will rejoice.

And those who have not left the flock,

nor ever forgotten the way,

still following Him,

must be ready to receive

the lost one that God returns today.

Lord, I could have been one

who became lost on the rough,
hard path so steep,

but You saw me falter

and lifted me up

into the center of Your faithful sheep.

Now that I am here, Lord,

and blessed amid Your flock, I pray

that You will use me

to help protect another wandering lamb

As You guide him back into Your way.

Renewal

Psalm 32:3-5 – When I kept silent, my bones grew old through my groaning all the day long. For day and night Your hand was heavy upon me; my vitality was turned into the drought of summer.

Selah

I acknowledged my sin to You, and my iniquity I have not hidden. I said, "I will confess my transgressions to the Lord," and You forgave the iniquity of my sin.

Selah

When I was overwhelmed by
my own sin, Lord,
I ran to You
And You were there and helped me out of it.
Even when I would return to my sin
again and again,
You were still there working to
rid my life of it,
Forgiving me in Your mercy,
In spite of my weakness,

Never letting me go altogether away

from You.

You held me firmly and You spoke

to my conscience

So that though I gave in

to my worldly desires

again and again,

I was never able to be content in it for very long,

And You made Yourself known to me

at every moment;

I could not escape Your Presence.

Now the sin has been rejected, put

forcibly out of my life,

And only You are to be praised for the

Working of Your will to my good end.

I had continually asked You, Lord,

to do this in the face of

my weak nature,

And You did it, and You brought healing

To others through healing me.

In this time, Lord, I have seen my imperfections

In contrast to Your perfect will

for me,

And I am reassured of Your great love

as my Father

Who has determined by Your grace

That I will be in Your Kingdom

at the end of my days.

Times of Temptation

It is so easy and tempting

To fall back into the weaknesses

That are part of the old me.

My Lord has freed me from these,

Giving me a wonderful new life.

But at times something pulls at me

To go back

And be what I used to be.

Full of jealousy, resentment, and self-pity,

Not compassionate, selfless, or patient.

Oh, God, help me to be

What You want me to be.

Only then will I be

Content and at peace.

The Burdens I Bear

I Peter 2:20-24 – For what credit is it if, when you are beaten for your faults, you take it patiently? But when you do well and suffer, if you take it patiently, this is commendable before God. For to this you were called because Christ also suffered for us, leaving us an example, that you should follow His steps:

> "Who committed no sin,
>
> nor was deceit found in His mouth. "

who, when He was reviled, did not revile in return; when He suffered He did not threaten, but committed Himself to Him who judges righteously; who Himself bore our sins in His own body on the tree, that we, having died to sins, might live for righteousness — by whose stripes you were healed.

> The years of my life are passing by
>
> And heavy at times is the grief.
>
> But never will spikes pierce my feet and hands,
>
> Nor will I hang on a cross to my death.

Never the burden of the whole world's sin

On my shoulders will I bear.

Carrying it all to the depths of hell

To save those who may not even care.

He bore the cross on which He would hang,

And feeling the terrible pain,

My Lord Jesus took the spikes
driven right through.

For my sins He suffered the shame.

All grief, though dark, is easy to bear

When compared to His death on that tree,

And the joy of His love overcomes every trial

As I remember what He did for me.

Feeling Humble

God heals us from illness;

He comforts us in grief.

He understands our weaknesses,

Our times of unbelief.

He forgives our many errors

And loves us as His own.

What have we to give to Him,

But to love and trust His Son?

Drifting Thoughts

God and Man

With silos stretching up from flat, open fields

    Or skyscrapers above the asphalt roads,

With steeples atop little country churches

    Or towering spires on city cathedrals,

Man's handiwork vainly reaches
from earth toward heaven,

    Never quite touching it.

With sunlit streaks through stormy clouds

    Or showers and lightening
    from rumbling skies,

With sun and dew of early morn

    And luminance of midnight moon,

In omnipotent ease, God reaches down from

    Heaven to earth

Touching and filling it with Himself.

Better or Worse

Hebrews 12:1–2 — Therefore we also, since we are surrounded by so great a crowd of witnesses, let us lay aside every weight, and the sin which so easily ensnares us, and let us run with endurance the race that is set before us, looking unto Jesus, the author and finisher of our faith, who for the joy that was set before Him endured the cross, despising the shame, and has sat down at the right hand at the throne of God.

Being a Christian is not being in a contest or race to see who can do the most or be the best as compared to those believers and non-believers around us. Instead, it is a one-person race against time, the time which we have left to live here in this world. Our individual goals are to become what God wants us to become and do what God wants us to do before our time here runs out.

In a race against time there are no winners or losers. One just constantly tries to improve the past record through training and practice until the goal is attained. For Christians, this training and practice is done partly by reading God's word, both alone and in fellowship with other believers. Also, we seek God's will by praying and then acting on His answers to our prayers as well as on the things we learn through study. The more we do these things, the closer we come to finishing our race and reaping the rewards.

God's Prophets

Mark 13:22 — For false christs and false prophets will rise and show signs and wonders to deceive, if possible, even the elect.

Who are Your prophets, Lord?

I want to beware of those

who come bearing words and ideas from men

instead of from Your Spirit,

who play on my worldly wisdom to cause me doubts

instead of pointing to God's way;

who gleefully flatter my pride in my works

instead of giving You the glory;

who sympathize with my self-pity

instead of encouraging me to give thanks in all things;

who push me to constantly do and hurry

instead of letting me rest in the Lord;

who, in false piety, hush my singing heart

instead of letting me find joy in praising you.

And I want to watch for Your true prophets, Lord.

I shall know them by Your love and through Your Spirit.

The World or God

The pleasures of this life are not what I'm after.

God's Kingdom is the goal for me.

To some others, I seem to have dropped out of the race,

But it's a different race in which I happen to be.

I could change tracks and attain the world

And all its excitement and fun,

But my joy will only be complete

If God's race is the one I run.

If I seem to be alone while others

With friends greatly abound,

I say I'd rather be alone with Jesus

Than to be just one of a crowd.

Many times I come to the point of wondering

If I'm wrong and these others know best:

That I should get away from this life I live

And join in the worldly quest.

Then God always finds a way to remind me

I'm not failing by the way He judges,

And if the world chooses to leave me behind.

I'll finish the race God has set before me

To attain a crown of a different kind.

Storms in Life

I do not pretend to know the why's about God. But this I do know: out of something fearful and dreadful to us humans, God can create something beautiful. That is to say, God has the power to change the worst of things into the best if He so chooses.

An example of this was a hurricane on the Texas Gulf Coast in the late 60's. It was Hurricane Beulah, which was predicted to come in with winds at 130 miles per hour or more. My husband and a friend were firemen who would undoubtedly be busy during the storm, and they sent the other wife, our collective seven children, and me to San Antonio to wait out the storm.

The winds were not as bad as predicted, but the heavy rain of a stalled storm wreaked havoc in the area. It seemed that an uncontrollable monster had poured his giant vats of water down until the Rio Grande was over its banks and the levees were in danger of giving way. One could not help noticing that even God's natural creation, as well as man-made structures, was ruined by wind and the hopeless flooding. There was the tragedy of lost and destroyed material possessions.

Weeks later, as men strived to rebuild their creations, God was effortlessly rebuilding His. Trees, which were left standing and weren't supposed to lose their foliage for several months, were stripped of their leaves and some branches by the winds, but now were putting on fresh green leaves. Flowering plants also were blooming. We, whom God loves, were treated to an out-of-season springtime.

Even though many people lost a great deal in the storm, I believe my faith was strengthened. Out of the storm, finally the sunshine returned. Out of the flood, other than damage for the present, water was plentiful for crops later on. Out of men's fear came compassion for others who had lost so much. God uses these storms to show us that He can easily repair what seems to be impossible to fix, and His beauty will shine through in the end.

Several years later, I had a storm in my personal life. Other smaller storms and their outcomes, just like Beulah, had been preparing me for this terrible one. God had strengthened me to be able to stand on his Rock through that turmoil. After the worst of it, at mid-life, I began to bloom out of season. The losses I suffered at the time one by one turned to sunshine, well watered soil, and new growth in God's Spirit. My fears turned to compassion for others in their storms. My life had never been better than it was at the end of my disaster. Everything that was taken from me was returned a hundred fold and more. I have learned not to fear the storms.

Psalm 89: 8) O, Lord God of hosts, who is mighty like You, O Lord? Your faithfulness also surrounds You.

9) You rule the raging of the sea; when its waves rise, You still them.

11) The heavens are Yours, the earth also is Yours; the world and all its fullness, You have founded them.

A Meditation on James 3:8-10, 14

James 3:8–10 —8) But no man can tame the tongue. It is an unruly evil, full of deadly poison.

9) With it we bless our God and Father, and with it we curse men, who have been made in the similitude of God. 10) Out of the same mouth proceed blessing and cursing. My brothers, these things ought not to be so.

14) But if you have bitter envy and self-seeking in your hearts, do not boast and lie against the truth.

Why is the tongue more dangerous than any weapon? God always provides the strength to overcome any temptation, so surely He will give us the strength and power to hold our tongues in check. Yes, He will do that, but the muscle that works my tongue seems to have the quickest reflex action of any muscle in my body. At the very instant a jealous, bitter, or mean thought enters my brain, it seems to be on my tongue, with the thinking process following minutes later. Most sins that we commit are weighed and rationalized before being committed, and we know ahead of time that we are about to perform that act. Not that we deliberately commit a sin, but at least before doing it, there is usually time to think about it and decide to do it or not to do it, considering the consequences that will follow. Not so with the tongue—the tongue depends almost entirely on what we have stored in our minds. In a world of instant foods, computers for instant solutions, prefabricated buildings, and speed travel, we should be able to understand the instant speech that is triggered by strong emotions and to know why it is so easy for curses and praise to come so quickly, one after the other, out of the same mouth. But even with this strongest of all magnets to evil action, there is a way to fight it, and God expects us to put up the fight with His help.

First of all, reflex vocal action comes from conditioning. So how am I conditioning my tongue? To begin with, it is conditioned by the direction of my thoughts I hold on to during quiet moments. I have control over the leisure dwelling of my mind on different ideas. During these quiet periods, if I focus my thinking on Godly things, then I begin a process of crowding out the debris of jealousy, hatred, bitterness, and lust. The more this trash is crowded out, the less chance it has of spewing out in a moment of emotional reaction.

But there aren't enough quiet times in today's busy lives to let those be the only times at which we consciously condition our thinking. We have to be concerned about the outer influences of our daily activities also. What we choose to see and hear in movies, T.V., and radio does much to add power to our reflex tongue action. So if my quiet times crowd out the trash, and then I turn around and bring in that same trash through what I allow myself to listen to or watch, what progress have I made? It's like digging a ditch, throwing out the dirt, and then shoveling the dirt behind me back into the ditch. I'll never get that ditch dug. Instead I need to throw each shovel full of dirt out of the area, up on the bank, far from the edge so it doesn't fall back in. I can do that by not watching or listening to anything that would be considered trash according to God's word.

Another way I condition my tongue is by choosing the places I go for recreation. Certain places are known to be filled with actions and scenes that God hates. Why make it harder on myself by deliberately inhabiting those places? If there is known to be dirty language, cursing, drunkenness, and promiscuity in a place, and if I'm trying to grow in the life God chooses for me, it would be foolish to deliberately put temptation of that kind all around myself. It is hard enough to fight the sinful nature within me without giving strength to my enemy.

Then there are those associations over which I have no control. In this world we can't altogether avoid outside influences. If we work for a living, if we go to school, in fact, in just living day to day in this world, we are confronted hour by hour with all kinds of people and situations that bring to surface our sinful natures. We cannot ignore the people we work with, go to school with, or meet in our daily living, but we can control how we see them. If I consciously look below the surface as Jesus does and love them as Jesus does, then in this act alone I am successfully repelling the wrong feelings and thoughts that could fill my heart through these daily contacts with life.

God helps us in our reflex actions of our bodies and especially our tongues through helping us to condition our thoughts. Seeking His power and strength through praying and reading His word as we come in contact with the world, this is the only way to turn these tongues into instruments of praise rather than damaging weapons against one another and against God.

Prosperity with God's Blessings

Psalm 127: 1—Unless the Lord builds the house, they labor in vain who build it; unless the Lord guards the city, the watchman stays awake in vain.

John 10:10—[words of Jesus] The thief does not come except to steal, and to kill, and to destroy. I have come that they may have life, and that they may have it more abundantly.

A person who prospers by doing what Scripture says he should not do is not being prospered by God, but by Satan. Satan delights in seeing anyone turn against God's laws and will deceitfully dangle all kinds of "goodies" in front of that person who has his eyes on fame and money instead of on Jesus. Yet it is well known that Satan is a killer, a liar, a thief, and a destroyer. He sees a gullible person, even one who claims to be a Christian yet who has his sights on money, and lures him on as that person thinks it must be God prospering him so well.

We would all do well to see where prosperity is coming from:

gambling, cheating, watching horoscopes, lying to ourselves and others, pushing others aside to get ahead, bribery, greed all are morally and scripturally wrong ways to prosper. A person may prosper by one or the other of these ways, but as with all of Satan's ways, they allow us to be deceived.

On the other hand, if we are prospering in spite of giving away what we have and it just seems to come back through opportunities opening up, through an insight that helps us see just the right and honest approach and not be afraid to use it, by allowing a "deal" to get away when it goes against Jesus' teachings about fairness and Godly love, by centering our thoughts on Jesus instead of on making money, then we can be sure this prosperity is from God and we can accept it, give Him the glory for it, and enjoy it as His gift to us. If God wants to prosper us, nothing can stop us.

We, then, have to be very cautious about believing we must be living right just because we are raking in the money. Satan has the power to give us riches when he realizes he can pull us closer to him by enticing us with them. We need to look at how and why we are making a success of what we do. If we are succeeding while getting farther and farther away from God's desire for us, we should beware. If we are so far away from God and so close to Satan, then Satan might answer our greedy prayers, not God. And if Satan is answering prayers, we are dangerously close to his becoming the one we worship and depend on for our help.

Remember, Satan is a thief who comes only to kill, steal, and destroy, so while he prospers a person for a while, it is only for his own purpose of finally destroying that person and others. On the other hand, Jesus came to give life and give it more abundantly, and prosperity through him will give good life to those about us and reflect back on us as from a mirror. If I must prosper by ways that hurt others or which go against God's laws, I would rather not have riches. If God wants them for me, He will show me the way, but it will be His blessing that gives them to me and not my own actions. I would rather prosper with God's blessings.

Whom Do We Worship?

The world was given to Adam by God when He told Adam to keep it and tend to it. All things were placed in Adam's charge. When Adam let the serpent, through Eve, tell him what to do, he let the serpent take charge over him. In that sense Adam delivered it all over to Satan, who kept it and its inhabitants, directing their thoughts and actions until the day Jesus rebuked everything Satan said to him [Luke 4:1-14] Jesus took charge, then, over Satan because He did not submit to his deception. He put Satan under His authority instead of coming under Satan's authority. Now we have a choice of submitting to Jesus or to Satan.

If I had the choice of submitting to a master who would beat me and cheat me or a master who would take care of all my needs and even invite me to his own feasting table, of course I would choose the latter. We have such a choice between Jesus and Satan.

Satan is still trying to strengthen his kingdom for the final battle, so he tricks, lies to, and cheats people into doing things against God's laws in order to get those people under his authority. He knows they will die in the battle to come at the end of time, but he doesn't care. He, the cruel master, continues to gather all for his own selfish, albeit futile, ends.

Those who have chosen Jesus as their master are not exempt from the trickery of Satan. But they are given the ability to recognize the signs of its being used on them. This ability comes through knowledge of the differences in God's way and Satan's, a knowledge developed by reading the Scriptures God has provided for us to use in battle. [Ephesians 6:10-117]

We do act constantly either on thoughts and ideas from God, or else from Satan. It is necessary to be able to discern from which source we are receiving ideas so that we are not cheated out of our places in the good Master's kingdom. It is necessary to read and read and read and digest fully the Word of God. That is our inoculation against the virus that Satan tries to spread among us.

A Paraphrase on Isaiah 58
Fasting

Fasting is scriptural; it is right. However, just as anything we do for good, it is no good without following God's basic laws to honor him and to do good to our fellow man. Verses 6–13 tell how:
When you fast,

　　　—be fair to those that work for you [or under you],

　　　—share food with the hungry,

　　　—give the shelter and love of your
　　　homes to the helpless and poor,

　　　—give clothing to those who would be
　　　cold without what you give,

　　　—take care of relatives who have less than you,

　　　—do not make false accusations or spread rumors,

　　　—help people in trouble, and

　　　—enjoy the Sabbath as the Lord's day and
　　　honor Him on that day with what we do.

The results will be that God will

       –heal you,

       –be your shield ahead and your protection behind,

       –answer when you call,

       –make light out of darkness for you,

       –continually guide you,

       –give all good things to you,

       –keep you healthy,

       –make you productive,

       –put your life back together, and

       –see to it that you have your full share of all His Blessings.

Hallelujah!

Thinking about December 25

Jesus, dear Jesus, is today the day of Your birth?

This we don't really know.

Yet we are sure that the Son of God

Was born to man many years ago.

Your Father gave You to this whole world.

It matters not what day;

The angels sang, and the shepherds came

As Your bright star lit their way.

That star led wise men from the East

In search of a new King Child.

They'd read the signs, and they found the King

In a place most humble and mild.

The stage had been set, as God had planned,

In Bethlehem, in a lowly stall.

Was it a place for a great King to be born?

'Twas the most unlikely place of all!

Yet, there, Your humble birth has shown

That the greatest gift one can bring

Is to share the gentle love You gave

As our Savior and our King.

The date is not important, but only that You came;

And even more important, still,

That You lived and loved and died for us

On a cross on a barren hill.

That You arose, defeating death for all,

Claiming victory in the end,

So we now live in blessed assurance

Of lives free and not condemned.

Now with Your gracious blessing,
we'll celebrate on this day

In honor of the day You were born,

Knowing this is just the beginning

Of celebrating the resurrection morn.

Prayers and Testimonies

Testimony

If "God so loved the world

That He gave His only Son,"

Then what am I to do

When the world denies what He's done?

Do I shout and loudly exclaim,

Condemning all I see,

Or quietly sit back in shame

In fear of our destiny?

I'll not fear being only one,

For God has a vast army:

Those He's called to be His own

And from the world's sin be free.

As one of this army of God,

I know words may meet deaf ears:

So I stand before the worldly crowd

With His Spirit to calm my fears,

Then with all His women and men,

I live my life by His guiding hand

"Til we reach a victorious end

As in obedience to Him we stand.

No, it doesn't take shouting to share

How His sacrifice lifted me

Above all the burdens and cares,

And this the world shall see.

When more than the words I say,

My life is the message I bear,

Then the sinful world of today

One by one may begin to hear,

As gently and in God's will,

I share Who makes my life so;

His Spirit leads them on until

To His Son they finally go.

A Guide for Life

Ephesians 6:16–17—above all, taking the shield of faith with which you will be able to quench all the fiery darts of the wicked one. And take the helmet of salvation, and the sword of the Spirit, which is the word of God;

Psalm 91:3–7—Surely He shall deliver you from the snare of the fowler and from the perilous pestilence. He shall cover you with His feathers, and under His wings you shall take refuge; His truth shall be your shield and buckler. You shall not be afraid of the terror by night, nor of the arrow that flies by day, nor of the pestilence that walks in darkness, nor of the destruction that lays waste at noonday.

A thousand may fall at your side, and ten thousand at your right hand, but it shall not come near you.

Psalm 91:11-12—For He shall give His angels charge over you, to keep you in all your ways. In their hands they shall bear you up, lest you dash your foot against a stone.

> If Faith I wear as my shield,
>
> And salvation upon my head,
>
> And the Spirit's sword I wield

When into battle I'm led,

No fear need I ever know.

As forward I march in His will,

Amidst arrows the enemy throws

I'll boldly cross the battle field.

Though thousands around me fall

His armor shall not fail me.

God is the Lord of all,

And His truth keeps his people free.

He has promised His angels' care

Keeping us along our way,

Helping skirt the enemy's snare,

And taking us through each day.

His Holy Spirit is nigh:

We need but listen and be still

Then lift His name on high

And joyfully receive His love

As we concede to Him our will.

Lead Me, Lord

Help me, Lord, to think about

what I do before I do it.

Help me think first of You, Lord,

then others, and last, myself.

First to ask, "Would my Father approve?

Would He be glorified?"

Then, "Would it help my brother

and draw him closer to God?"

Or "Would it drive him far away?"

And last ,"Would I be burdened with

guilt when it's all done?

Or would I know that I had tried

to stay within my Father's will?"

Oh, let my thoughts, my
actions and words,

reflect Your wondrous love

So those around me feel it too,

Your Spirit from above.

Reflecting God

Psalm 119:10–16— With my whole heart I have sought You; Oh, let me not wander from your commandments!

Joshua 1:5 — No man shall be able to stand before you all the days of your life; as I was with Moses, so I will be with you; I will not leave you nor forsake you.

I would not want to turn
away from you, Jesus,

For never have You turned from me.

You are with me in the bearing
of life's burdens __

I want to be with You in
bearing the cross.

You are with me in feeling life's joys__

I want to be with You in the
joys of serving our Father.

At all times, in all places You are here.

Let me be with You as You are with me.

He Lets Me Know

Isaiah 1: 2–4— Hear, O heavens! Give ear, O earth!

For the Lord has spoken:

"I have nourished and brought up children,

And they have rebelled against me.

The ox knows its owner,

And the donkey its master's crib;

But Israel does not know,

My people do not consider."

Alas, sinful nation,

A people laden with iniquity,

A brood of evildoers,

Children given to corruption!

They have forsaken the Lord;

They have provoked to anger

The Holy One of Israel,

They have turned away backward

When I mourn because of my nation's
turning away from the Lord,

He shall show me the beauty of the
miracles of His universe:

> —the blazing sky of His sunset,

> —His rays of light through morning clouds,

> —His rainbow after a storm,

> —geese in their ordered flight to other regions,

> —a butterfly recently reborn from its cocoon.

Then I have hope.

In my mourning He pours over me His healing oil

And I find joy

> —in friends who have become my family in Him,

> —in His word that speaks of
> His everlasting presence,

> —in serving whomever He sends to me,

> —in feeling His Spirit covering me,

—in the light with which He surrounds me.

And I am drawn out of my mourning,

From my heaviness of heart, and He
fills my mouth with praise,

And I am aware

    —that He is merciful to forgive,

    —that He wants all men to come to Him,

    —that He sees a fallen sparrow,

    —that He is Almighty God,

    —that He is the Beginning and the End.

Then my burdens are lifted as I give them all to Him,

And pray, knowing His anger with our nation will end

When we come to Him and repent, and turn back

To Him, in faith,

And our nation will be healed.

Holy Spirit

Father, You put Him in my heart

To guide and protect and set me apart.

May I not grieve Him in any way,

But always may I let Him have the say.

In all I speak and all I do,

May my life be pleasing to Him, and to You.

If this is how I live for all my days,

Joy will shine in me like the sun's bright rays.

Thank You, Father, for giving to me

Your Holy Spirit, who keeps me free.

Song of Life

Light and life are mine to keep

Though death may lay me down to sleep,

For my Lord has promised this to me:

Life in Him is for eternity.

Death cannot take my life away

When I walk alive in Him each day.

His Spirit in me lingers on;

The body's life is all that is gone.

Nothing hinders, nothing binds

As His love my spirit finds.

He lifts me up and I don't die,

For in His hands my life now lies.

Death may remove me from this place,

But with death, at last, I'll see His face.

Joy fills my heart because I know

His mansion awaits me when I go.

This is no morbid song of death;

It is a song of life and breath,

His resurrection gave this to me,

A song of life for eternity.

Prayers and Counsel

God's Nourished Seed

Send Your rain, Lord,

To soften the soil of their hardened hearts.

Send Your laborers, Lord,

To till the ground and plant Your good seed.

Send Your sun, Lord,

For them to be wrapped in its loving warmth.

Let Your rains come, again, Lord,

To break away the stubborn clods of their minds.

Let Your sprouts come forth, Lord,

And break away their imprisoning shells.

With Your rain and sun to enrich, Lord,

And Your laborers to tend them daily,

Your seeds in the hearts of these blessed ones

Will flourish and grow toward heaven,

And the glory of their ripened fruit

Shall be the glory of Your redeeming love.

Do Not Wait Too Long

She was suddenly gone.

    A quiet person,

    unassuming;

Nonetheless, she had been there,

    always there.

Her presence noted

    in her shy smile

    and a soft "Good morning."

She slipped in and

    Slipped away

    Sunday after Sunday,

    perhaps unnoticed

Except by those

    who knew and loved her,

who depended on her,

who knew how she served the Lord.

I did know her, though not well.

I did care but never told her;

I hoped my outstretched hand

on Sunday mornings

Told her I cared.

That's all I did;

Should it have been more?

Why do we let people

Slip into and out of our lives,

Never telling them "I care,"

if we really do?

To reach out a hand,

That is good,

But to reach out one's heart

in friendship

through a call,

a visit,

a few words:

"I was thinking of you."

"Let's have coffee."

"May I come to see you?"

That is how to really care.

"Inasmuch as you did it

To one of the least of these My brethren,

You did it to Me."

The words of Lord Jesus

Still speak.

To heed them,

That is the secret of true service,

True love as He taught it.

The loss of someone we care about

Is a hard way to learn.

To a Grieving Friend

You are grievous and sad

With all that's gone on,

Loneliness and grief

Your only song.

If only I could help you

To see down the road,

How God and time

Can lift the heaviest load.

There's light to be found

In this old, dark world

As faith and hope

In God are unfurled.

He blesses and comforts

As no one else can;

You have but to ask

And reach for His hand.

It's always outstretched

And calling to you.

He'll be father and mother,

Brother and friend, too.

It's hard to imagine

How this could be,

But I'm able to tell you

It's happened to me.

So laugh when you can

And cry when you must,

But remember God's love

Is worthy of your trust.

I'm hoping and praying

You'll reach for the best

Put your hope in God

And He'll do the rest

The Beauty God Sees

God sees beauty that men can't see.

He sees it where it is buried deep.

He gently tends it, and from its sleep,

The beauty He sees begins to be.

The glow, the tenderness that begins to show

In the eyes, in the touch, in the warm soft smile

Is not just there for a little while,

But lasts long past youth; through age it grows.

And then one day beneath a silvery wreath

The Godly face of an aged saint

Shows radiant, and no longer buried deep,

The beauty emerges softly, as a new spring leaf.

It has surfaced now and by all is seen

And they wonder at that face and the way it glows

With the love and gentleness and serenity bestowed

By God through years of His Spirit within.

A Mother's Wish Granted

One day one of my daughters was having a particularly bad day with her children. She was thinking out loud about how nice it would be some day when she didn't have to go through all the difficulties of tending to all their needs and their spats with each other and how she would someday have time for herself when they were grown. We talked about it, and after I went home, I sat down and wrote this sad poem. I've never been sad about my children having grown up, but I'd not take anything in trade for the precious moments that filled in the gaps between problems when they were small. I, too, had those moments of frustration during those years when they were small.. Children can give joy or sorrow at whatever age they are, but I have found that if I can give thanks just for the fact that God gave them to me, the sorrows grow dimmer and the joys radiate even more until those joyful moments are what I remember now. And the children grow ever more loving toward each other as well as toward me and toward God in time. These are the real blessings we seek in the gift of our children, aren't they?

At the end of one day, an ordinary day,

When the children were still quite small,

She sat in her chair and
dreamed of the way

Her life would be when they were tall.

"No squabbles," she thought,
"no taunts or tattles,

The peace will soothe my ears

No drying of tears, no settling of battles,

Oh, hurry and pass, you years!"

Then another day, another ordinary day,

When the children had all grown tall,

She sat in her chair and
pondered the way

That time had stolen them all.

She found herself to be quite alone

While silence and peace did abound.

The tears that she dried
were now her own

For having lost what she'd never found.

Evening Magic

Evening makes any season more beautiful.

A stark bare sight

Of leafless trees

Is velvet crewel

In winter twilight.

New green of trees and grass

In springtime,

With late day sun,

Becomes green stained glass.

In summer, white hot hues

Of burning hot skies,

With evening breezes,

Become cool grays and blues.

And the most beautiful of all:

Dying leaves

Blaze alive

At sundown in the fall.

CPSIA information can be obtained at www.ICGtesting.com
Printed in the USA
LVOW130231280313

326379LV00001B/2/P